A HOME IN THE BIOME

At Home in the
OCEAN

Louise and Richard Spilsbury

PowerKiDS press™

New York

Published in 2016 by **The Rosen Publishing Group**
29 East 21st Street, New York, NY 10010

Produced for Rosen by Calcium
Editors: Sarah Eason and Amanda Learmonth
Designers: Paul Myerscough and Emma DeBanks

Picture credits: Cover: Shutterstock: Rich Carey; Insides: Dreamstime:
Aquanaut4 15, Mirage3 12–13, Worapat Maitriwong 17, Peternile 27, Thijs
Schouten 22–23, Stammers 16–17, Vitalyedush 4–5, Jeremy Wee 5,
Whitcomberd 14–15, Xvaldes 11; Shutterstock: Ricardo Canino 25, Rich Carey
13, Ethan Daniels 9, 10–11, pan demin 1, Jubal Harshaw 7, Natalie Jean 8–9,
Juancat 18, Vladimir Melnik 23, Christian Musat 18–19, PawelG Photo 6–7,
David Persson 28–29, Stefan Pircher 26–27, Travelmages 20–21, Kirsten
TsuneoMP 24–25, Slateterreno 28, Wahlquist 21.

Cataloging-in-Publication Data
Spilsbury, Louise.
At home in the ocean / by Louise and Richard Spilsbury.
p. cm. — (A home in the biome)
Includes index.
ISBN 978-1-5081-4573-8 (pbk.)
ISBN 978-1-4994-1856-9 (6-pack)
ISBN 978-1-5081-4567-7 (library binding)
1. Marine ecology — Juvenile literature. 2. Marine biology — Juvenile literature.
3. Marine animals — Juvenile literature. I. Spilsbury, Louise. II. Spilsbury,
Richard, 1963-. III. Title.
QH541.5.S3 S75 2016
577.7—d23

Manufactured in the United States of America
CPSIA Compliance Information: Batch BW16PK: For Further Information contact
Rosen Publishing, New York, New York at 1-800-237-9932

Contents

At Home in the Ocean

The world's oceans cover more than three-quarters of Earth's surface, so they are an incredibly important biome. From the shallow waters near coastlines to their deepest, darkest depths, the oceans are full of life. Yet this biome has some serious challenges for the wildlife living in it.

Light and Dark

Although it is light at the ocean's surface, it gets darker and harder to see the lower down you go. It also gets very cold in deep water. The waters of the ocean are very salty, which is why we cannot drink seawater. Another challenge is that ocean waves can be very strong and wash plants and animals away if they are not **adapted** for life in the sea.

The largest animal in the oceans is the blue whale. A blue whale can grow to 100 feet (30 m) long because its weight is supported by the ocean water. It has a thick layer of fat called blubber to keep it from getting too cold. It has excellent hearing to help it find its way in the dark, and to find food.

The blue whale's broad, flat tail moves up and down to help it swim through strong waves.

Plankton

The waters at the surface of the world's oceans look clear and empty, but in fact they are full of plankton. Plankton is the name given to the collection of different kinds of tiny animals, plants, and bacteria that drift along in the water and are carried from place to place by the ocean currents.

Plant-like Animals

Some plankton are forms of algae. Algae are like plants because they use energy from sunlight to turn **carbon dioxide** into sugars they can use to grow. The tiny creatures in plankton include the **larvae** of animals such as crabs and jellyfish, and shrimp-like animals called copepods. Animal plankton feed on the plants or other **microscopic** animals that form part of the plankton.

This magnified view shows plankton of all shapes and sizes. There are thousands in a single drop of water.

HOME SWEET HOME

Some plankton are flat and round; some have spines or hairs. They have different shapes and features to help them float near the water's surface, where they can get the light they need to make food. Some plankton can glow in the dark! They give off a blue light to scare away or confuse **predators**. When many plankton glow together, we can see them.

Kelp

Giant kelp is the largest seaweed in the world. This enormous plant grows in areas of deep water near coasts. Seaweeds need light to make their food, like the plants that grow on land. A variety of animals live, feed, and have their young among thick forests of kelp.

Reaching Toward the Light

Kelp has long stems and leaf-like parts called fronds that are adapted to reach up to the light at the water's surface. Kelp has long, branching stems that can be up to 130 feet (40 m) tall! Kelp stems have to be very strong to cope with the strong ocean currents that pull them around in the water.

Giant kelp seaweeds have air-filled compartments at the base of every frond. These act like floats to help the fronds reach the sunlight at the surface.

HOME SWEET HOME

Kelp is anchored to rocks on the ocean floor by large, root-like parts called holdfasts. These hold kelp onto the rocks even in strong waves. The kelp stems grow up from the holdfasts at a rate of up to 2 feet (60 cm) a day!

Jellyfish

Jellyfish are not really fish at all! Jellyfish are soft-bodied sea animals that live in oceans all over the world. They mainly travel by floating along on ocean currents.

Trailing Tentacles

Jellyfish have long **tentacles** that hang down from the bell-shaped part of their body. The tentacles trail along below them as the jellyfish drift in the water. When the tentacles touch a small animal, such as a fish or crab that is passing by, they release a sting. This keeps the animal from moving. Some stings can even kill the animal outright. Then the jellyfish moves its **prey** toward the mouth in the center of its body, and eats it.

Jellyfish can move by opening their bell (the large, round part that forms the top of their body) and filling it with water. Then they squeeze their body tight and push out the water. This makes them move quickly forward, like a balloon when air is pushed out of it.

Jellyfish do not have eyes or ears. They have cells that can sense light, and smell and taste things. These sense cells help them find their way and find food in the water.

Sea Turtles

Sea turtles waddle slowly on land but they are excellent swimmers. They move their wide, flat flippers to help them swim and dive deep down below the surface to find food. Their hard shell protects them from many ocean predators.

Tearful Mealtimes!

Some turtles eat jellyfish. Sea turtles get water as well as food from their prey. A turtle's body removes salt from the water inside the jellyfish by emptying the salt into its eyes. When the turtle comes ashore, this salty water oozes out of its eyes and it looks as if it is crying!

Sea turtles use their front flippers like paddles or oars to pull them forward. They use the back flippers for steering. Sea turtles have a strong, hard mouth shaped a little like a bird's beak to grab jellyfish and other prey.

HOME SWEET HOME

Female sea turtles swim onto sandy beaches to lay eggs. They dig holes in the sand with their back flippers, lay eggs in the holes, then hide the eggs with sand. The baby turtles hatch out of the eggs and crawl along the sand to the ocean.

Sardines

Sardines are small, silvery fish that feed on plankton as they swim along. Like other fish, sardines have gills to breathe underwater. As water moves over the gills, oxygen passes into the fish's body.

Safety in Numbers

Sardines travel together in large groups called shoals. This protects them from ocean birds, **mammals**, and other fish that try to eat them. These predators may be confused by the large number of sardines. If a predator cannot spot one particular fish to chase, it may not be able to catch any of them. At night, the shoal sometimes breaks up to look for food, but it always gets together again in the morning or when a predator comes near. A shoal of sardines may contain up to 10 million individual fish.

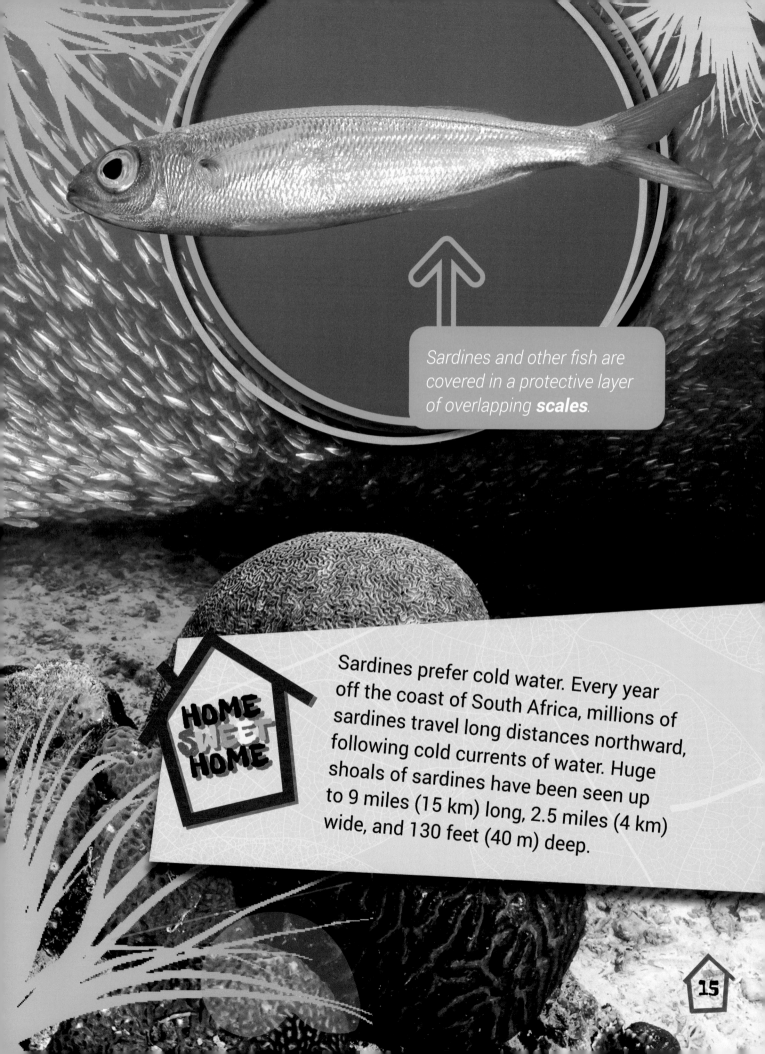

Sardines and other fish are covered in a protective layer of overlapping **scales**.

HOME SWEET HOME

Sardines prefer cold water. Every year off the coast of South Africa, millions of sardines travel long distances northward, following cold currents of water. Huge shoals of sardines have been seen up to 9 miles (15 km) long, 2.5 miles (4 km) wide, and 130 feet (40 m) deep.

Stingrays

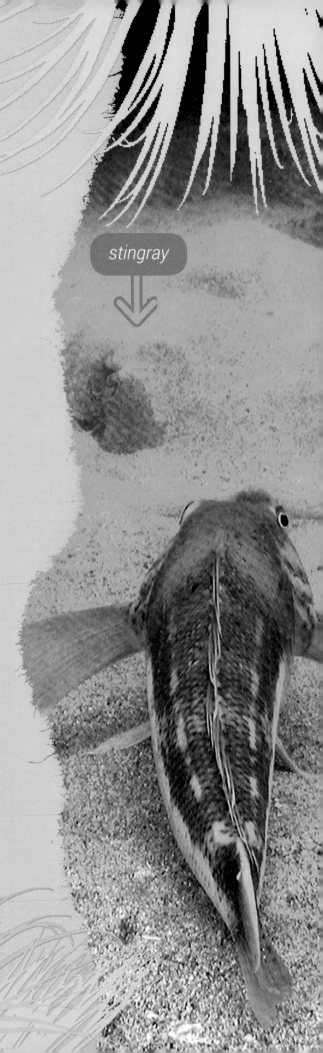

stingray

Stingrays are designed for life on the ocean floor. These unusual-looking fish have very flat, wide bodies and they spend most of their lives lying on the seabed. Their eyes are perched on the top of their bodies so they can see what is going on above them.

Can You See Me?

When a wide, flat stingray lies still on the ocean floor it can be hard to see it! The skin on a stingray's back is colored and patterned to look like the ocean floor. This **camouflage** helps it hide from predators and catch its prey. The stingray lies on the seabed, partly covered in sand. When a fish, crab, clam, or other prey comes along, the stingray swoops over and bites into it with the hard mouth on the underside of its body.

Stingrays swim gracefully through the ocean by gently flapping their wide pectoral (side) fins up and down, a little like wings.

HOME SWEET HOME

A stingray has a long, whip-like tail with a sharp and jagged spine on it. If something disturbs a stingray, it whips its tail to attack. Some types of stingrays have poison in the spines that can kill an animal almost instantly.

17

Penguins

Penguins spend most of their lives by, or in, the ocean. They have feathers, wings, and a beak like other birds, but penguins cannot fly. Instead, they use their wings for swimming.

Made for the Water

Penguins can see better in water than they can on land. Most penguins have sharp beaks that are useful for grabbing slippery prey, and some even have tongues with backward-pointing spikes that keep caught fish from escaping. Penguins drink seawater and then get rid of the salt from a special part in their beaks.

18

HOME SWEET HOME

Penguins have a thick layer of blubber to keep them warm in cold water. They also have two layers of feathers. The top feathers are oily and form a waterproof coat. The lower feathers are short and fluffy and trap heat. Penguins have wings that are smaller, stiffer, and flatter than most birds' wings, and shorter feathers. Penguins use their wings like flippers to push against the water. They use their legs, feet, and tail for steering.

A penguin's **webbed** feet push against the water when it swims, and help the bird walk on snow and ice.

Sea Otters

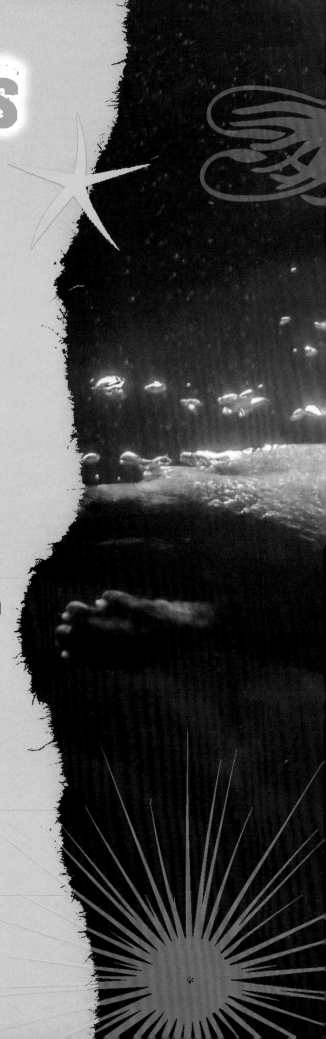

Sea otters are brown, furry mammals that live in cold waters near the coast. They dive underwater for up to five minutes at a time to find food. Sea otters swim using their wide, webbed back feet like flippers. They also twist their strong tails from side to side to help them swim.

Life in the Water

Sea otters eat a variety of animals, including sea urchins, snails, starfish, and octopus. To find their prey in dark water, sea otters use their whiskers to feel the **vibrations** made by moving animals, and use their paws to feel along the seafloor. Sea otters have two layers of thick fur that trap air to keep them warm, and also help them float. Sea otters usually sleep at the ocean's surface, floating on their backs. They roll and twist in kelp to keep them from drifting away while they are sleeping.

A sea otter eats its food at the ocean's surface by floating on its back and using its stomach as a table!

HOME SWEET HOME

Sea otter mothers rest their pups on their stomachs and float on their backs to keep the pups out of the freezing water. Pups also have a special fluffy coat of fur that keeps them warm and acts like a life jacket to help them float. At two months old, the pups learn to swim and dive for food for themselves.

21

Walruses

Walruses are amazing ocean animals. These large, strong mammals are as big as a small car and have a pair of huge white tusks that can be up to 3 feet (1 m) long!

Icy Ocean

Walruses travel and feed in the icy waters in and around the Arctic, and then come up to rest on the ice or land. They have a layer of blubber up to 4 inches (10 cm) thick to keep them warm. They use their wide legs for swimming and they can dive underwater for 10 minutes at a time before coming up for air. They feed on animals such as clams, mussels, and crabs, which they catch on the ocean floor. Walruses use their long whiskers to feel for food on the ocean floor.

Walruses spend two-thirds of their time swimming and feeding, and about one-third of their time resting or sleeping on land or ice.

HOME SWEET HOME

Walruses use their tusks like ice picks. They stick the tusks into the ice to get a good grip, and then haul themselves out of the water and up onto the ice to rest. They also use their tusks to bash a hole in the ice when they want to get back into the water.

Dolphins

Dolphins spend their whole lives in the ocean. These beautiful, intelligent mammals have a long, narrow shape that helps them speed through the water. They use their strong tails to help them swim fast, and their flippers and fins to steer them through the water.

One Big Pod

Dolphins live in groups called pods. Pods hunt for fish together. Hunting in teams helps dolphins catch more food in the huge oceans. Dolphins communicate with each other using sound, because sound travels well through water and because it is hard to see other dolphins in deep, dark water. Dolphins make sounds by forcing air through tubes inside their noses. They can make about 30 different noises, including whistles, squeaks, and grunts!

Dolphins have sharp, pointed teeth for catching their prey.

HOME SWEET HOME

Dolphins use **echolocation** to find prey in deep, dark ocean waters. First, they send out a lot of clicking sounds. When the sounds hit an animal such as a fish, echoes bounce back to the dolphins' ears. The dolphins can tell where the fish is by figuring out where the echoes come from and how long it takes for them to return.

Great White Sharks

The great white shark is named for its huge size and its white belly. This shark has an incredible sense of smell. If a fish or other ocean animal is injured, the shark can smell even just one drop of blood from far away. Such adaptations make it one of the ocean's top predators.

Hidden Hunter

The great white shark's belly helps it hunt. As it swims along searching for food, animals that look up from below cannot see the shark because its white belly blends in with light shining into the ocean from above. Animals swimming above the shark do not see it when they look down because its gray back blends in with the darkness below.

Sharks swim quickly when they are on the attack. Their bodies are long and thin to help them cut through the water and swim fast. The side and back fins help them steer and stay upright in the water. They move their tail fins from side to side to travel forward.

The great white shark's huge mouth is full of razor-sharp teeth that can bite through the skin, flesh, and bone of tuna, dolphins, and birds.

Oceans Under Threat

There is a great variety of wildlife in the world's oceans and we rely on the ocean for many things, including the fish that we eat. However, the ocean faces threats from people. When people pollute the ocean with litter or things like oil and waste, this can harm ocean wildlife. Giant fishing boats also take more fish from the oceans than the fish can naturally replace. When people take too many fish from the sea there is less fish for other ocean animals to eat, and some types of fish are now in danger of dying out.

When people catch too many fish, there is less fish for other ocean animals, such as monk seals, to eat.

Protecting Our Oceans

Around the world, people are trying to protect ocean biomes. They study oceans to see how changes affect wildlife there. Governments make laws about how many fish people can catch. They create reserves, which are areas of the ocean where wildlife is protected. **Conservation** groups also raise money to help protect **endangered** ocean animals, such as the Hawaiian monk seal.

HOME SWEET HOME

The Hawaiian monk seal is endangered for several reasons. Some starve because there are fewer fish for them to eat, and some are killed to keep them from taking fish that people want to catch. Some get tangled up in fishing gear, and drown.

Glossary

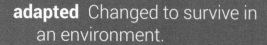

adapted Changed to survive in an environment.

bacteria Tiny living things too small to see. Bacteria can cause disease.

biome A community of plants and animals living together in a certain kind of climate.

camouflage A color or pattern that matches the surrounding environment and helps an organism hide.

carbon dioxide A gas in the air we breathe. Carbon dioxide is also found in water.

conservation The act of guarding, protecting, or preserving something.

currents Movements of large areas of water.

echolocation The use of echoes to find things.

endangered When a plant or animal is in danger of dying out.

flippers Wide, flat limbs used for swimming.

gills Body parts that fish and some other animals use to breathe underwater.

larvae Animals at the stage when they have just hatched out of eggs.

mammals Types of animals that feed their babies with milk from their bodies.

microscopic Something that is so tiny it has to be viewed through a microscope.

oxygen A colorless gas in the air we breathe.

pollute To put something harmful into water, air, or land.

predators Animals that catch and eat other animals.

prey An animal that is caught and eaten by other animals.

scales Small, overlapping plates of hard material.

tentacles Long, flexible structures on an animal, a little like arms.

tusks Special large teeth.

vibrations Shaking.

webbed Having skin between toes or fingers.

Further Reading

Bedoyere, Camilla. *Monsters of the Deep*. Richmond Hill, ON: Firefly Books, 2014.

Ganeri, Anita. *Ocean* (Lifesize). New York, NY: Kingfisher, 2014.

Ocean: A Visual Encyclopedia. New York, NY: Dorling Kindersley, 2015.

Oliver, Clare. *Oceans* (100 Facts You Should Know). New York, NY: Gareth Stevens Publishing, 2014.

Reynolds, Tony and Calver, Paul. *Ocean Life* (Visual Explorers). Hauppauge, NY: Barron's Educational Series, 2015.

Websites

PowerKids Press has developed an online list of websites related to the subject of this book. This site is updated regularly. Please use this link to access the list: **www.powerkidslinks.com/ahitb/ocean**

Index